Real People. Real Stories. Real Help.

A New Normal

Learning to Live With Grief and Loss

Darlene F. Cross, M.S., M.F.T.

Darlene Cross, M.S., M.F.T., Inc.
Las Vegas, Nevada

A New Normal: Learning to Live with Grief and Loss

Published by

Darlene Cross, M.S., M.F.T., Inc.
www.darlenecross.com

ISBN 978-0-9843441-0-9

Book design and layout by Robert Goodman, Silvercat™, San Diego, California

printed in the United States of America

With deepest gratitude and appreciation for Gary Gardia, LCSW, my mentor in the world of grief and loss work, and my relentless muse in writing this book.

And with unconditional love for the two greatest teachers I have ever had, my sons, Jason and Brandon Cross.

You may be certain that if you want to be a pilgrim, you are going to get lost. The old Boy Scout manual offered some practical wisdom for those who are lost on any quest. First, don't panic. Second, stop doing what you were doing. Third, sit down and calm yourself. Fourth, look for landmarks. Fifth, follow trails or streams that lead downhill or toward open space. A mountain man was once asked if he often got lost. "No," he replied. "I've never been lost. But sometimes for a month or two I didn't know how to get where I was going."

from *Fire in the Belly: On Being a Man,* by Sam Keen

CONTENTS

Introduction

Have you experienced the profound loss of someone dear to you? Are you feeling helpless, numb, overwhelmed, maybe disoriented as if nothing around you makes sense anymore? You may even be embarrassed you are so emotional, or not emotional enough. Or maybe you are like I was, struggling to gain a foothold after my own first significant loss when I didn't know which way to turn first.

I knew I wasn't the first or the only person to experience the unexpected death of someone so dear, but that's exactly how it felt. The questions I had then are the same questions people have been bringing into my therapy practice now for over a decade. People from all walks of life with all types of losses have the same questions and the same need for information.

That's why I wrote *A New Normal*. You have likely found books of inspiration, books offering quick and easy solutions on how to "get over it," when what you need are respectful and practical answers. You want information that helps you make sense out of what you are thinking, feeling and experiencing. You want a book that helps you know what to DO!

Inside *A New Normal*, you'll discover how to understand what is happening to you, where you are in your grief process, and what you can expect as you go forward. You will learn that it is okay to give yourself permission to grieve, that grieving is part of being human, and that while grief is universal each loss is unique.

You will meet other newly bereaved people in *A New Normal*, including some interesting characters that will prove that YES, you can still laugh. You will gain tips along the way and get plenty of practical proven ways to navigate through your grief and your loss. You will see that grief is normal. Once you understand how it works, the process can be a little less painful and a lot more productive.

I never had any ambition to write a book. This book gave me no choice, it demanded to be written! It is the book I never found when I needed it most. It is the book I want my loved ones to have when the day comes they need it most. If the insights and stories you are about to read help you understand one thing you didn't understand before about your loss, if your pain is lightened even the slightest bit, then this book will be a success.

You've waited long enough in this place where every minute is an eternity. It's time to take back your life, time to work with your grief in a way that honors both you and your loved one. Let's get started.

NOTE: All stories in this book are based on actual cases. All names and some details have been changed to protect the identity and confidentiality of the people involved.

Chapter 1

Making the Grief Process Work for You

Does it seem impossible there could be any way to make sense of the chaos you may be experiencing after the death of your loved one? Have you heard advice you question? Have you read materials that left you with more questions than you had before?

In this chapter you will learn how to recognize what is happening to you. You will gain knowledge that will begin to make some sense from the senseless, giving you a greater feeling of power in a powerless situation. And, you will see how grieving after a loss is a very normal human experience no one gets to escape.

Am I Normal?

If you are feeling confused and disoriented after your loss, then you are right on track. Even your body may feel like it no longer belongs to you, and your mind has temporarily left the building. While these feelings would be troubling in your every day life, they are very normal when you have experienced a significant loss.

The normal reaction to witnessing or learning of the death of a loved one is shock. Your mind fights to grasp some semblance of reality, at the same time rejecting the reality that has from one moment to the next completely changed your world forever.

As normal as experiencing shock may be, it can interfere at critical moments with your ability to react as you ordinarily would. What could be more disconcerting than to open your mouth and have nothing come out when you are desperate to speak? How frustrating is it to pick up the phone to dial home in an emergency only to find you have forgotten your own number?

Shock is the culprit when everything around you seems to be moving in slow motion. Your body feels like it weighs a thousand pounds; every breath takes effort; words just don't work the way they should. The famous Salvador Dali art that portrays an assortment of drooping, dripping and distorted clocks is a perfect image of this phenomenon and suggests the artist may have known this subject all too well.

Shock is a normal reaction to a very abnormal situation, your body's way of protecting you without a single conscious thought. The slowing down of your thoughts and actions are in effect allowing you to process threatening information in a way that is designed to maximize your own chances for survival. Viewed this way, you can see how shock is an incredible coping mechanism, your best friend waiting patiently to help you when you need help most.

Ann's Story—Did Ann Fail Her Loved One?

Ann's husband of over 50 years had an inoperable aneurism. They both knew for years the aneurism could rupture at any time, immediately ending his life, or it might never rupture at all. This advance knowledge did nothing to prepare Ann for the day when "never" ceased to be an option.

The couple was spending a quiet afternoon at home. Ann walked into the kitchen for a drink of water, only to find her husband in the throws of what could only be a ruptured aneurism. She knew she should get help but found herself unable to make even the slightest movement. She stood frozen in horror as the man she loved died right in front of her eyes.

When Ann came to therapy, she explained that she knew there was nothing that she could have done to save her husband's life. She was deeply appreciative of the time she did have with him, more than she had expected. What she was struggling painfully with was the fact she had not acted more quickly at the time, unable to do something as simple as go to the phone and dial 911.

My Comments to Ann

Ann listened intently as I explained to her what was happening to her body physically in this time of crisis and why she had been unable to function. She sat quietly for a few moments, looking down, considering the information. She looked back up at me and she asked, "You mean that was my body keeping me safe?" I assured her that it was. She reached back to pat her own shoulder and with a big smile said, "Thank you, Body!"

Nature is determined to maximize the odds that you will survive, even the toughest of situations. Reacting with shock means you are automatically functioning at your best when you have been challenged with the absolute worst.

Stages, Formulas, and Blueprints—BEWARE!

You will likely see many books, models and blueprints about grief that may not work for you. It can be very frustrating to try to fit into a plan that simply does not fit your needs and may create more obstacles than you already have.

The most widely known model you have likely heard about is commonly referred to as the "stages of grief." This theory describes a progression of predictable stages of emotions in how you can expect grief to behave. You may be wondering what stage you are in or can expect to soon experience, or if you are doing it "right." Keep reading because the shocking truth is, there is no such thing.

So much has been written and said about the stages of grief that the concept has become urban legend. What was originally intended to help terminal patients understand their emotions somehow over time morphed into a model of how grieving people could expect their emotions to behave. What may have appeared to be a helpful model for grieving only proved to confuse and mislead, but the concept is not likely to disappear anytime soon. I even saw an employer who used the stages model to teach managers how to give a negative performance review, as if the experience could be effectively compared to dying!

The truth about grief is it does not come in stages, the process is not linear, and recurring emotions are very much a part of the experience. It is not like a train ride where you check off stations you visit on the way to your destination when your trip finally comes to an end.

Grieving comes in cycles, likes waves in the ocean. You can be standing calmly one minute at the water's edge. A wave then comes along that rocks you gently off balance but you quickly regain your equilibrium, no harm done. Then, you bend over to examine a pretty shell that catches your eye, and just when you least expect it you are knocked over by a wave crashing into your behind and filling your nose full of water while you struggle to catch your breath. That is what grief is really like.

Grief—Friend or Foe?

Grief is powerful. It affects you physically, spiritually and emotionally. The indisputable fact is grief will make its demands on you. No one gets a free pass when it comes to the emotions of saying good-bye to someone you love. The choice you do have is whether to work with your grief and allow it to help you through your pain, or resist while your pain patiently follows you around sneaking into unexpected places until it can demand your full and undivided attention.

A New Normal Tips

Trust Your Body. If you need to sob, sob for all you're worth and don't care who might hear. If you are okay for the moment and want something to eat because you feel a little hungry, head for the fridge.

Know Emotions Are Fleeting. If you have just destroyed your favorite pillow in a fit of rage and feel a sense of relief, do not be fooled into thinking you are done with anger...or that the rest of your pillows are safe.

Avoid Amateur Experts. If you find yourself the recipient of free advice, keep what works for you and throw the rest away. If you don't want any advice, it's okay to interrupt and change the subject. And always remember the only expert on YOUR loss is YOU.

No Short Cuts and No Free Passes

Just as there are no quick or easy steps to an imaginary finish line with grief, there are also no free passes. Some argue that they are fine and do not need to grieve, declaring they just need to get on with their life.

Tom's Story—Did Tom Get a Free Pass?

Tom was an older gentleman attending his first session of a bereavement group for widows and widowers. One participant had just shared a particularly emotional memory that deeply affected everyone in the group—except Tom. He sat quietly throughout the meeting until his silence became awkward and he spoke up.

Tom said that he had fought in World War II. He proudly stated soldiers were taught not to feel emotions. Not only could he not allow or process his own emotions over his wife's death, he was nearly crawling out of his skin to even witness the emotions of others. Tom quickly switched the subject to moving on and how he planned to join a singles group to start dating, even though his own loss had been quite recent.

Tom never returned to the group and no one knows what happened to him. What is obvious is that ignoring his emotions did not mean he didn't have them, and no one will ever know the price he paid for holding them inside.

YES to Emotions, YES to Life!

An argument can be made for getting on with life as usual after experiencing the death of a loved one and not allowing emotions to rule, but at what price? Being turned off to hurtful emotions means you are turned off to happy emotions as well. Rejecting emotions is anything but getting on with life, rather it is avoiding it. Emotions come in all shapes and sizes and experiencing the entire range is living life fully, through the good times and the bad, and everything in between.

Understanding the cycles of grief means knowing that feelings will come and feelings will go, and that both are absolutely normal. Your body knows how to grieve, even if your mind does not. Trust your process. Embrace your feelings, knowing some day the hurt will be a little less making a little more room for the joy found in cherished memories.

Now that you realize you can't control or program or escape your grief, are you ready to start working with your grief process? In the next chapter you will learn the skills that will help you say goodbye to your old normal and hello to your *New Normal*.

Chapter 2

Good-Bye to Your Old Normal

Now that you know grief is a process, you may wonder where the process begins. What is the first step to creating your New Normal? Your journey starts with what is possibly the toughest task of all, the non-negotiable job of letting go of your old normal.

This chapter will explore what is happening to you in the initial days and weeks following your loss. You will also learn some practical things you can do to help yourself through this difficult time.

Letting Go of What?

Letting go of your old normal is not the same thing as letting go of a person. What does it mean if someone says to you, "You have to let Sam go?" Maybe you aren't ready to let Sam go. Maybe you don't want to let Sam go. Or maybe you don't even believe it's possible to let Sam go because Sam lives on in your heart and your memories that you don't ever want to let go.

Does this mean you flunk "letting go?" Is it any wonder you are confused about exactly how or if to let go?

Rather than letting go of the person, in this example Sam, what you can let go of is the life you had before Sam died. Your old normal life stopped with Sam's last breath. It is not negotiable, it is not a choice. It is most likely not something you want to do, rather it is something you must do.

The more you resist your new reality, the harder the process will be for you. The more you accept and allow the process of letting go of your old normal, the more energy you will have to cope with your loss. And the good news is you don't ever have to let go of someone you love, you just keep them in a different place.

A Death-Denying Culture

It doesn't make saying good-bye any easier when we live in a culture that minimizes, denies and sometimes considers death downright inconvenient.

The denial of death is imbedded in our every day language with sayings like, "I could have just died," or "It scared me to death," or "I nearly had a heart attack." You may have surprised yourself when a death-related cliché slipped out of your mouth after your own loss and you froze mid-sentence.

Then there is the rude and inconsiderate truth that life does go on. Your landlord may express condolences over your loss but still expects the rent check on time. The electric company won't even bother with condolences; pay up or lights out. A generous employer may give you a week off work, but you will be due back the following week ready to resume normal duties.

You Aren't Sick, You Are Grieving

It seems like every time you turn on the news these days, there is some new report exaggerating facts in favor of theatre. Even simple, every day emotions are often given mental health diagnostic labels, as if there is something pathological about feelings. Grief is simply an emotion, and grieving is the normal reaction to losing someone you love.

The most normal thing in the world is for you to want your life to go back to the way it was before your loss, to turn back the clocks to before they were drooping. You may try to return to your old normal, knowing that the only thing you can go back to is a normal routine. Re-establishing your routine is in fact helpful in coping with your grief, but should never be confused with believing your grief is finished.

You aren't just saying good-bye to someone you love, you are also saying good-bye to your normal way of living and being. Virtually every area of your life is impacted, starting from the moment you open your eyes every morning and continuing through to the end of your day. And just as you may be struggling to accept the loss of your old normal, your New Normal is already making demands you cannot ignore.

Pauline's Story—Did Grief Find Pauline at the Grocery Store?

It had been only three short weeks since Pauline's husband died. The guests and the mountains of food that came with them were all pretty much gone, and it was time to go to the grocery store. Pauline's routine for years had been to go to the store every day to choose the freshest ingredients she would use to prepare the evening meal, only this day would prove to be very different. She went into the produce section and was busy picking out the two best baking potatoes she could find when the shock of her reality hit—she only needed one potato. Who would have thought a potato could mean so much? Using her delightful sense of humor to help her through her pain Pauline declared, "From now on I'm buying potato salad!"

I Wasn't Prepared For That!

You may think it's a strange comparison to consider experiencing your first traumatic loss as kind of like falling in love for the first time, but the two have something very much in common. As a human being, you were born with the capacity for love and the ability to grieve loaded into your hardware, but it seems there's been a serious design flaw because no one loaded the software!

The first time you fall in love and the first time you experience a major loss, you are completely overwhelmed and clueless about how to proceed or what to do with your flood of intense emotions. While falling in love is arguably more enjoyable than grieving, recalling a first broken heart can be an emotionally packed trip down Memory Lane. You do eventually learn how to deal with your emotions, but the first time can be the most challenging.

A Year of Firsts

Most grieving people will tell you the first year is the hardest. It is a year filled with holidays and birthdays experienced for the first time with the ominous absence of the person who died. The first year of grief culminates with what is often the hardest of all, namely the first anniversary of the death. Subsequent years continue to be a challenge, but the feelings tend to be less raw when they are more familiar.

You muddled through your first love, and your first heartbreak, only to become stronger, more experienced and more resilient. There were likely other heartbreaks along the way, but none that left you as lost as the first. It may be hard to think of grieving as a learned skill, but in many ways that is exactly what it is.

A New Normal Tip

Be Prepared For Special Days. Anticipating upcoming events that may provoke heightened emotions can be the best defense. Maybe you buy you mother's favorite flowers and place them by her picture for Mother's Day. Maybe your Thanksgiving family dinner includes stories of feasts shared in the past when your father was present. Maybe you include his favorite dish in his honor, or maybe you choose to retire it since he isn't there to enjoy it. Pretending everything is the same when it is not tends to make special days so much harder when they are already hard enough.

The Gift of Clarity

Life never seems quite as clear as when you view it from the perspective of death. It reminds you that you don't have forever to do the things you want to do. Death can make wasted time and opportunities look foolish and every minute valuable, every relationship precious.

You may find your values shifting. You recognize more easily what is important and discard what is not. You may decide to quit that job where you have been so unhappy for too long. You may decide to terminate an unhealthy relationship. You might even decide to go back to school to get that degree you've always wanted. Creating a New Normal isn't easy, it isn't quick, but long-term results can be more than worthwhile. What a testimony to the unending value of your loved one in your life!

What Do I DO?

First, give yourself a break. You will tend to sleep poorly, dream actively, and disappear into daydreams often. You may find yourself being difficult, short tempered, and with no patience for anything or anyone. Maybe you prefer to withdraw into your own private world in the early days following your loss. Maybe you need to surround yourself with people and avoid being alone. Any and all of these behaviors are normal, even typical, for someone who is newly grieving.

People in pain can easily fail to recognize their own needs. You really can be too physically and emotionally depleted to know what you need or want. To make matters worse, you may have to take on a whole new set of unexpected responsibilities. Maybe you have to cope with a pile of legal paper work you don't understand. You may have to pack up a house that is full of memories, and by a deadline you didn't choose.

You might be worried about how you will pay unexpected bills. Is it any wonder you're exhausted?

Go with the Flow. Know that you are going to miss your loved one for the rest of your life. Why wouldn't you? You don't "get over it," you learn to live with it, one minute, one day, one year at a time.

Take naps. If sleeping in your own bed is difficult, try sleeping somewhere else for a few days. Changing routines, even for just a short time, can be helpful when normal routines are difficult.

Assign jobs you need done when people ask what they can do. Give them a task even if it's just to keep them from hovering. Let them do the laundry or wash the dishes or run the vacuum. If they didn't want to do it, they shouldn't have asked!

Tell people if you need alone time; tell them if you don't. Don't let others tell you what you need as if they know better than you do. They don't.

Walk your dog. Talk to your cat. Don't be surprised if the animals are better listeners than the humans around you.

Journal or write letters to the person who died. It is okay if what you write is angry or sad; it's okay if it is not. Just write. If writing isn't helpful to you, don't write.

Design your own rituals. Rituals can be a powerful tool when you are struggling to access or process your own emotions. Consider using music, flowers, candles, photos, treasured keepsakes.

Let your emotions out. The more you resist, the harder it gets. Grieving is deeply primal. Don't be afraid to let it look and sound and feel that way. You may want to do this work in private with doors and windows closed so you don't feel the need to monitor your own behavior and to avoid interruptions from worried pets or nosey neighbors.

Reject shaming advice that "you should get over it" or "you should move on." Unsolicited advice is not the same as asking for input or an opinion that you want and ask to receive.

Be real. The fact someone else "has it so much worse" may help you put your loss into perspective, but it does not make it any less significant. No two losses are ever exactly the same. Your pain is your pain, and their pain is their pain, and an exact comparison of losses is not even possible.

Fight the need to DO SOMETHING NOW. You may be very tempted to sell your house, get cosmetic surgery, or join the Peace Corp. Think twice before making any unnecessary major changes for at least the first few months, and maybe even as much as a year. You want to make changes because they are best for you when they are best for you.

Be gentle with yourself, give yourself time. Know the day will come when you will feel better, but that day isn't this day.

No one is a true expert on grief. Unfortunately at some point, we all become experts of our own individual loss experiences. There is no one who can know what is best for you better than you.

You now have knowledge that grieving is a normal human process in an abnormal situation. You know that life as you have known it is irretrievably changed forever. Are you ready now to learn how the type of loss you have experienced impacts the development of your New Normal?

Chapter 3

Understanding Impact from Types of Loss

Have you experienced an anticipated loss, or a sudden loss? Maybe you learned of a loved one's illness or injury only to lose them before you even had time to deal with the initial news. Do you wonder how each affects people who are grieving—people like you?

In this chapter you will learn about the differences between types of loss. You will gain knowledge of what makes anticipated versus sudden loss different from one another, and what you can expect to experience from each. You will read ideas and suggestions of what has worked for other grieving people to help ease you through your own loss.

The First of Two Evils—Predictable Loss

It is a very different experience to witness the dying process of a loved one from a terminal illness than if that same person were to die suddenly. Knowing someone you love is dying gives you choices, as difficult as they may be, while losing someone without warning gives you few.

An anticipated death allows friends and family to come together in a supportive and loving community. It gives you and your loved ones a chance to say good-bye in what can be a very healing and even beautiful experience. Some have described being present at a loved one's passing as a more spiritual experience than giving birth.

Having time to say the things you want and need to say, or simply to listen when a dying loved one speaks can be deeply meaningful. Every minute, every word, and every action can be profound as memories are created to ease you through the difficult days ahead.

Amy's Story—Can a Few Words Really Be So Important?

Amy lay in Intensive Care, unable to speak, after what would ultimately prove to be a fatal stroke. Struggling to get a message through to her family, she finally wrote a note in barely legible handwriting. Her last written request she worked so hard to deliver? "Please let work know I won't be there." An impeccable work ethic to her final days, Amy was easily reassured by her loving children that the call had already been made. And then she rested. As is so often the case, small things really do mean so much.

My Comments on Amy's Story

Often well-intentioned loved ones will reassure the patient that everything will be all right and that they are going to be fine. Maybe it's because they believe it's true, maybe it's because they want it to be true, or maybe it's because it makes them feel better to say it. Regardless of the reason, the problem with minimizing the seriousness of a life ending, or potentially life ending situation is that the patient's wishes may not be heard, may even be dismissed. Had Amy's children not been willing to listen rather than reassure, they may never have known what was so important to their mother or been able to act on her behalf in a way that meant so much to her.

Bumps in the Road

Of course, not all expected deaths or the situations surrounding them go smoothly. If the dying person was difficult to deal with when healthy, they can be more than a challenge when they aren't. And if family relationships were tenuous before, as illogical as it may seem, a death in the family can bring out the worst in some survivors.

The death is about the person who died. Your emotions are about how you handle your loss, and other mourners' emotions are about how they handle their loss. Keeping the focus on the person being honored at the end of a lifetime can put things into perspective during times that may challenge you the most.

Mary's Story—No Good Deed Goes Unpunished

Mary was a kind and generous woman. After her mother's death, she took over the role of caregiver for her more than cantankerous old grandmother. Nana was famous for being a master manipulator, often using guilt and a sharp tongue as her favorite weapons. It was clear she had received better than she had given.

Nana's always difficult personality became even more challenging when the time came that Mary was no longer able to care for her at home. Despite many years of selfless devotion to Nana's care, Mary felt that she should do more and tried to figure out a way to rescue her from the care facility.

My Comments to Mary—Trading Guilt for Peace of Mind

I asked Mary what had happened that prevented her from bringing her grandmother back home to live. She explained how Nana had collapsed and all her bodily functions had failed. She shared that even the paramedics struggled to move her from the home to the ambulance. Efforts to stabilize Nana in a care facility resulted in her being moved back to the hospital each time, finally being placed on hospice care.

I asked Mary what other possible options she had in caring for Nana, and she was clear there were none. We discussed Nana's toxic words. After examination, Mary realized that Nana's words were nothing but mean, intended to injure. Nana's accusations weren't even true and the only thing that gave them power was Mary's reactions.

Mary traded guilt for the peace of mind that she had done her best and would no longer let Nana's words wound her. She felt comfort in the knowledge her mother would have been proud of her for giving so much to someone she knew was so difficult.

The Conclusion of Mary's Story

Mary continued to visit Nana every day. As she was leaving one evening, Mary said, "Good-night, Nana. I love you. See you tomorrow." And the old woman let loose.

"It's your fault I'm here. You could take me home if you wanted. See me tomorrow? I may be dead by tomorrow!" Mary calmly looked at her grandmother and said, "Then I won't see you. I love you, Nana. Good night." Mary completed therapy with flying colors.

Proactive Grief Is a Thief

Proactive grief means you withdraw from the patient, from your loved one, by distancing yourself both physically and emotionally. This is an effort to avoid the pain from knowing a loss may be imminent. You may or may not be aware of your behavior, and you could even feel guilty for your choice of actions. You may visit less often, keep yourself busy with distractions, or find excuses why you aren't available. When you are there, you may feel anxious and find yourself chattering about mindless subjects or staying busy with meaningless tasks.

While your reactions may be normal, the problem with proactive grief is it is a thief. It robs both you and your loved one of the precious little time you do have left. It gives you only one choice and takes all others away forever.

Staying present and focused demands your strength and your courage, but the rewards can be great. You are completely present with and for the person you love while they are still with you. No matter how long we have with someone we love, it is never long enough. There will be plenty of time for grief all too soon.

The "D" Word

The "D" word—death, dying, died, dead—the proverbial elephant in the living room. When someone is dying, often people are afraid or just don't want or know how to talk about death. It's as if using the words has the power to provoke the very thing you want to avoid.

If you find yourself in this situation and don't know what to do or say, there's good news. You don't have to say anything, just LISTEN! If the person who is ill needs and wants to talk about death, providing witness can be a gift from you to your loved one. You may even be amazed at what you hear!

What Do I DO When Someone I Love Is Dying?

Allow yourself to participate in your grief community, those around you who share your loss. Tell stories, share memories, cry and laugh together.

Take turns sitting with the patient. Allow each caregiver time together and rest time alone.

Do not try to fix the problem. This is not a puzzle to be solved; it is an experience and a process to be lived.

Know that just because a death is expected, it doesn't mean you shouldn't feel sad. Even when a death seems to be a relief for a suffering loved one, it is still normal to be sad and feel the vast emptiness that is left behind.

Realize the impact on your life if you were the primary caregiver. The patient likely became the focal point in your life, you always the vigilant protector of the patient's well being. Your 24/7 role changes to zero instantly, demanding a major life adjustment on top of your grief. Expect to be beyond physically exhausted after a long period of poor quality and frequently interrupted sleep and performing the intense demands of care giving.

Do not blame yourself if your loved one passes the one minute you have left the room. There are many theories about why this happens, but the fact is, it happens. Focus on the times you were there and not the one minute you were not.

The Other Evil—Sudden Loss

Sudden loss is a trauma, an assault to all senses, to your emotional, physical and spiritual well being. From one moment to the next, sudden loss changes your world forever.

Your brain is slammed into shock. Food in your stomach instantly sours. You may fall to your knees, completely unable to support your own weight. The desperate need to do something is trumped only by the fact you are powerless to do anything at all.

There is simply no way to prepare for this type of loss. Etched into eternal memory is that one phone call, that ominous knock on the door, that impersonal but too-familiar image on the 6 o'clock news. Your mind is screaming, "THIS ISN'T HAPPENING!" when clearly your body knows it is.

Reactive Grief

Reactive grief is ruthless. It is demanding, inflexible, and it is relentless. It discriminates against no one. There is nothing that can be said or done to change what has happened. Actions don't matter. Words of comfort mean nothing.

Whatever you need to do to survive is exactly what you need to do. In the initial hours and days, you may be blasted with the need for quick decisions that must be made when you are in no condition to make them. You may hear words that shock your senses, even in your numbed state of being. You may find yourself overwhelmed with tasks that must be completed when all you can do is sit quietly and shake your head in disbelief.

What Do I DO After a Sudden Loss?

Understand that if you are breathing and walking at the same time, you are doing GREAT.

Let professionals help. People trained in how to handle high stress situations can be a great resource when you and others around you find yourselves struggling to cope.

Make the necessary phone calls sharing the bad news, if possible. This can help begin to bring some reality to your situation, allow you to feel somewhat productive, and pull your support community together quickly. If you don't want or can't make the calls, assign the job to the person you want to do this for you.

Call the experts. You may be required to make some big decisions in a short period of time, and possibly in areas where you have little or no expertise. Estate attorneys, financial advisors, hospice staff, counselors, funeral directors can all provide critical and skilled information. Choose someone you feel confident will act in your best interest and let them do what they are there to do.

Do not be fooled by superficial kindness from the media. If they are there, it is for no reason other than the story. Try to be as boring as possible.

Somewhere In Between

Did you get news that a loved one was sick or injured and in only a little time they were gone? While this type of loss may be antici- pated, it definitely fits the patterns of sudden loss. Events blur from one reality to the next, with you just trying to keep up.

This type of loss can be even more difficult if the illness or injury was not considered to be potentially fatal. Loved ones are left behind to second guess their choices, choices made based on incomplete and inaccurate information.

"What If" Game

Sudden losses set survivors up for endless rounds of "What if…" and "If only…" Questioning yourself and playing out scenarios that might have yielded a different outcome is only natural, but it can also be frustratingly counterproductive.

You can ask yourself an infinite number of these questions, but they are questions without answers. You can never know for sure what would have happened with any of your hypothetical situa- tions. Go to the doctor sooner to get an earlier diagnosis of can- cer? No guarantee of a different or better outcome. Change doctors sooner than later? Same thing.

"What If" questions only get asked when something bad happens. Good results get taken for granted. You would never comment to your family, "I'm sure glad we left the restaurant when we did so we could make it home without getting into an accident!" Wouldn't that be silly?

With your growing knowledge about how grief works, how your old normal is in the past, and how different types of loss impact reactions, it's time to fine tune your loss experience. Are you ready to look at specifics on how your relationship to the person who died may influence you?

Chapter 4

Loss by Type of Relationship

Was your loss a parent? A sibling? A friend? Have you considered how your specific relationship to the person who died might be affecting your grief? Maybe you are struggling to put your present feelings into perspective compared to other deaths you may have experienced in the past. You might be trying to support someone you love who is grieving, searching for the right words to say or the helpful thing to do.

This chapter examines some of the more common losses most of us will experience at some point in our lives. Entire books have been written on each one of these losses alone, but here we briefly consider what makes one different from another and how they may be affecting you.

Parent Loss

The knowledge you will likely out live your parents does not seem to do much to prepare you for the eventual reality. Your age at the time of your parent's death yields very different effects. The quality of your relationship to a deceased parent also plays a key role in how you experience your loss.

Young Child Loss of a Parent

It is always hard to explain death to a child, even if it's a gold fish on its way to eternity via the toilet. Truthful and age appropriate answers work best. If you aren't sure, let the child ask questions to guide you through the answers they need and are ready to hear. Then, ask the child to explain back to you what they heard to make sure the communication had the desired result.

A three-year old demanded (as only a three year old can do) an immediate answer to his question. "Where is he?" Rather than try to explain death to a small child, his grandmother asked, "Where do YOU think he is?" The frowning boy thought for a moment and then broke into a big smile. "I think he's in the moon and the stars." That seemed as good an answer as any.

Talking to children about death almost demands some creative communications. However, care should be exercised in limiting the use of magical answers and stories designed to appease young children's concerns and questions. Adult logic and the pure, simple logic of a child are not remotely the same.

Alice's Story—The Dangers of Magical Thinking

Six-year-old Alice's grandfather had just died after a lengthy battle with cancer. Caring friends and neighbors worked to reassure Alice, saying that Grandpa was an angel now. They told her he would always be with her and would look out for her for the rest of her life. All she had to do was talk to him and he would hear every word. Visibly troubled, Alice was not remotely comforted by these words.

A few days after the death, a family member found a letter of confession the grandfather had written as he was dying. He admitted to his family that he had sexually molested his granddaughter, Alice, and several other young girls. The family members were understandably devastated and immediately sought counseling together and individually for Alice.

Alice came into the therapy room agitated and anxious. She did not make eye contact and stayed distracted by fidgeting with toys in the room. Finally settling down, she looked up with unforgettable giant blue eyes. Summoning up great strength and courage for such a little girl, Alice gave voice to her terror. "Now that he's an angel, he can find me and hurt me whenever he wants."

Instead of the idea of Grandpa as an ever-present being offering comfort to young Alice, the idea brought sheer horror. Who would literally think an angel could follow you and hurt you whenever it wanted? A six year old who trusted the adults around her to take care of her and tell her the truth.

Older Child Loss of a Parent

Adults will often isolate children from death-related events in an effort to protect them. These are irreversible decisions made with surely the best of intentions, but the results may yield less than desirable results.

Nikki's Story—Lost in Time

Nikki was a 30-something woman coming to therapy after a series of failed relationships, all with endings she had initiated. When asked for some details on her family history, Nikki shared she was only eight years old when she lost her father to a sudden death. She began to sob, rocked back and forth, held herself tightly and worked hard just to breathe.

Nikki described having been called to the principal's office where her uncle was waiting to take her home. She knew she must have done something horribly wrong for her uncle's unprecedented visit. His ominous silence on the drive home just proved she had to be in really big trouble. Nikki was more confused when they arrived at her house and her parents were not there. Her uncle flatly told Nikki that her father had died, that Mommy was resting, and that she needed to be a good girl and go to her room and do her homework.

When Nikki's father died, she was developmentally at an age where dads walk on water and can do no wrong. From that point forward, no man Nikki ever met came close to measuring up to the ultimate gold standard, namely her dad. Nikki was an adult still struggling to understand what she did wrong that memorable day, believing events beyond her control were her fault. Inside her adult body was a very sad little girl.

Efforts to protect Nikki from catastrophic events in this case clearly did more harm than good. No one will ever know exactly how the outcome would have been different had other choices been made, but including and reassuring Nikki rather than isolating her could have done nothing but improve the long-term outcome.

Teen Loss of a Parent

Losing a parent as a teen can propel a young person into adulthood quickly and way ahead of schedule. Treating the teen like a child at this critical time will likely result in resentment and rebellion, making a bad situation worse.

On the flip side, telling an adolescent boy who has just lost his father he is now "the man of the family" places a burden on the boy that is far beyond his reach and his role, and at the worst possible time. How could a boy even know what that means? This seems to be an assignment given only to male children. Have you ever heard a girl being told she is now "the woman of the family?"

Has the teen been allowed to make choices and participate in events surrounding the death? Has the teen been asked in what ways he or she would like to participate, or not participate? Involvement in the planning, rituals and the support network can be healthy and empowering for a young person who is grieving.

Adult Loss of a Parent

The affect of parent loss on us as adult children is complicated, at best. It comes with layers of meaning and emotional effects based on the quality of the relationship over the course of your lifetime.

You may experience little emotion with the death of a parent with whom you were not close. On the other hand, you can be beyond devastated after the death of a cherished parent; a loss that can take years to assimilate because the absence is so significant. You could even be surprised to find yourself processing strong feelings, ranging from love to hate, for a parent with whom you had a conflicted relationship.

One reaction that does seem to be universal when looking at the world for the first time with no living parent somewhere on the planet is the introduction to your own mortality. People of all ages describe themselves as "orphans." You are now the oldest living generation.

Spouse Versus Partner Loss

Losing a spouse affects every single aspect of your life, from the jewelry on your finger, to the way you fill out forms and pay taxes. Even friendships you thought would never change often do when you are no longer married, through no fault or choice of your own.

Couples who have shared their lives, but never legally married, emotionally experience loss just as deeply as those who did marry. However, acknowledgement and support of the loss of a relationship never legally sanctioned can be very different. Forms still get filled out the same way as before, tax status does not change, and being single again does not seem to be validated by the outside world.

Harry's Story—Invalid and Invisible

Harry and Linda had been happily together for many years. They had a healthy relationship, a loving family, a beautiful home, and owned a successful business together. Both having experienced prior divorces, neither felt particularly motivated to get married or make it a priority. Legal chores got put off indefinitely, including creating wills.

Linda was out enjoying her favorite hobby one day, flying her small plane, when a freak accident ended her life. When the authorities called the family with the news and immediate tasks that had to be addressed, they did not call Harry.

Linda's relatives made all the decisions and all the arrangements for Linda's funeral and resolution of her estate. Harry was relegated to the role of observer and friend of the deceased.

Harry's Therapy

Despite the pain of losing his beloved, Harry found peace of mind in that she died doing what she loved to do most. Harry was coping well with his reactions to the trauma and the overwhelming financial challenges he was left to face. What Harry struggled with most was being treated as if the most significant relationship of his life was invalid and insignificant.

My Comments on Spouse Versus Partner Loss

I have had the opportunity to work with many bereaved partners over the years, but very few spouses. The theme of exclusion is common in many of these cases. It seems that the support systems available to widows and widowers are more common and more widespread, possibly making the need for therapy much less.

Sibling Loss

The original love-hate relationship, we were stuck with each other from the moment the younger sibling entered the world. Siblings help us learn how to be in the world, how to share, how to resolve conflicts, and how to love someone we may also want to choke. On some level, we thought they'd always be there, until one day when they weren't.

Again, age at time of loss plays a key role. A small child who wishes away a cute baby brother may be certain his bad wishes had something to do with the baby's death. Add only a few years to the clock and the older sibling would likely never give a thought to the possibility of his wishes having any power to actually cause a death. Add a few more years and the older sibling would know that if all of us who have younger siblings could have wished them away when we were little, there probably wouldn't be any little brothers or sisters left.

Until more recently, books and research on sibling loss were all but non-existent. It was almost as if surviving siblings had been forgotten. When you consider the family hierarchy, it's easy to see how a sibling can fall in place behind parents, spouses, and children, pushing a key relationship pretty far down the list. New research and expanding publications offer increasing recognition and help with this major type of loss.

Friend Loss

Who do you turn to when you lose a good friend? This was the person who you told your deepest darkest secrets, someone who really knew you, shared your laughter and your tears. This was the person you could always count on to be there for you. This is the person you chose to be family.

Ideally, the relatives of your friend acknowledge and honor the important role you played in their loved one's life. Hopefully you are welcome as a member of the bereaved family. Unfortunately, this is not always the case. The family may not even know you or recognize you in the crowd.

In reality, you may be the best person in the entire world to know your friend's wishes and beliefs. You may be a connection for your friend's child or children to share stories and memories of their loved one like no one else can.

Find where you fit in, where you are welcome and needed, and where you want and need to be. If necessary, consider a separate celebration or private memorial with other friends who share your loss. If you are alone in this loss, maybe you have your own private funeral just for you.

Pet Loss—A Silence So Loud

Did you ever think a house could be so quiet? Where are the jangling tags? What would you give to be able to shush a bark or trip over a silly toy? How about another sloppy kiss received with feigned disgust?

For those of us who love our animals, when we lose them we are losing a member of our family. The grief is just as real and can be just as deep as it is for any human loss, sometimes even greater.

Never before have we lived our lives in such isolation, many even living the dream of working from home. Visiting a friend or relative now often means getting on an airplane instead of just jumping in the car to meet for lunch. We sit in front of our computers doing "social networking," and more of us are living single than ever before. Is it any wonder our pets have become so important? This is love that is constant, undemanding, and unconditional. How could the loss not be profound?

This is a time to surround yourself with the support of other animal lovers who empathize with your pain. Don't try to explain the loss of your four-legged family member to someone who does not share your values because it will only frustrate you. These are often the people who suggest you get a new puppy, or a kitten. They may even show up with what they consider to be a perfect replacement. Telling others around you that you need time to grieve and to heal before you consider adopting another member into your family can be a good way to shut down good intentions and prevent bad results.

You now have a perspective on your grief process. You've considered the degree of change that has occurred in your life. And you have a greater understanding of how the relationship to the person who has died may affect your emotions. Next we look at complications that can occur with grief and loss that may not be anticipated or recognized, but greatly impact your experience.

Chapter 5

Complications on the Way to a New Normal

Have you found yourself blind sighted by how far the effects of your loss can reach? Maybe you thought you were through the most difficult days only to be surprised when more of these days show up, where and when you least expected them.

Now it's time to look at the chronic after effects of loss. These are the recurring, often unexpected challenges of coping with loss that linger long after the funeral. This is the stuff most people around you never think of, and you are seldom allowed to forget.

I Quit

Grieving is hard work. It is a full time job and this employer is demanding. There is no time off for good behavior, no vacation earned for all your hard work and long hours, and your resignation will not be accepted.

Imagine a job where you are required to work every day around the clock without a single day off. You may get an occasional break, but then it's right back to work. Picture yourself waving good-bye to your co-workers as they head off for a fun weekend while you sit there all alone, doing your best to keep going. It isn't fair, it doesn't feel good, and it's exhausting. That job is called Grief.

It's Raining Losses

A graduate student writing a paper on grief contacted me for an interview. She asked good and thoughtful questions, and the time flew by. With five minutes left, she said she had one more question. "Is there any such thing as secondary losses?" I told her we should have taken five minutes to talk about grief, and the rest of our time to discuss secondary losses.

Secondary losses are all the new and additional losses that result from the primary loss, the loss of a loved one. They are largely why we don't just "get over it," because there isn't just one "it."

Parents who lose a young child, for just one example, do not only suffer that loss. The future they expected and planned for is gone. Lost is the possibility of any grandchildren from that child. Where is the smiling face of that handsome adult son when you celebrate your Golden Wedding Anniversary? The list of losses is endless.

The pain of secondary losses can occur even if you were not present or actively involved with the original loss. An infant's parent can die without causing any immediate conscious effect on the child. Yet, as that child grows, the impact of the parent's absence grows, too. It starts in Kindergarten when kids ask where your mom or dad is. It's there when that proud face is missing in the audience when you star in the school play, when you graduate from college, and on your wedding day. The list is endless because the losses are endless.

Secondary Losses are Sneaky

Just about the time you start to feel your New Normal settling in, the future comes sneaking up on you. The full realization that this life change is permanent begins to sink in. Whether you like it or not, life starts to change as new things happen and new events occur.

Fay was buying a car after her old one had been damaged in an accident. She was pleased with the great deal she was able to negotiate for a fabulous new car on the last day of the year. She went to remove her belongings from the old car, preparing for the exchange, when out of the blue Fay was caught completely off guard with an overwhelming rush of emotions. Suddenly, it hit her. She was surrendering the car that drove her dear one to the hospital one very dark night, a car ride that proved to be the last he would ever have. Unable to contain her heartache, embarrassing or not, right in the middle of a car dealership, she began to cry.

Now, you might think it's silly, even ridiculous to cry over a car, especially when you're getting a really cool brand new one. But, it was never about the car; it was about what the car represented. Trading the old car for the new was indisputable proof that life and time go on. It was about losing one more piece, one more connection to someone already too far away. It was about more sadness, when it was least expected.

A New Normal Tip

Expect the unexpected. Know that secondary losses will continue to occur indefinitely. Some of your responses may be expected but many will be a surprise. There is nothing wrong with you, even though at times you may feel like there is. The more you resist or ignore, the tougher the work tends to be. The more you go with the emotions, let yourself feel what you feel, the sooner you will be back on your path, moving forward to A New Normal.

What Do Dirty Laundry and Unresolved Grief Have In Common?

They both pile up. And at some point in time, they both can be pretty difficult to ignore.

When you experience a new loss, it's inevitable that you will compare the new loss to losses you have experienced in the past. The reactions and emotions become increasingly familiar despite the fact each loss is unique. You may find yourself surprised how a new loss can tap into any unresolved issues you may have with a prior loss, issues you may not have realized remained.

Even if you have managed to hold your grief at bay, the accumulation still occurs. Significant losses that have not been grieved may be tucked away on some shelf, but eventually the shelf tends to get too full and comes crashing down. Even a small loss that may seem relatively insignificant can be enough to trigger an avalanche of stored-up emotions.

Steve's Story—The Cowboy and the Baby Chick

Steve was a strapping middle-aged cowboy, tough on the outside and tender in the middle. He was in therapy dealing with some relationship issues, but one day he arrived with a very different problem. He was distraught. This big, strong guy was in tears as he shared the news that his dog had just killed a baby chick.

It was touching to see how much this man cared about animals, but at some point the grief seemed to be disproportionate to the event. Steve had grown up on a farm with lots of animals and surely this could not have been the first time he'd witnessed a farm animal tragedy. It seemed like something else must be going on.

Searching, I asked Steve if anything else had happened that day or if it was a birthday or anniversary of any significant day or event. He seemed perplexed at the question and thought about it for a long time. Finally he said that it was the anniversary of his brother's death, a death he had never faced, let alone grieved. I asked him if he thought it was possible that his brother's death might have something to do with the painful emotions he was facing that day. Without hesitation, shaking his head, Steve said, "Nope."

Closure Confusion

What does it mean? What does it look like and how do you get it? How do you know that you have it? Is it a good thing or a bad thing?

The concept of closure is another example of a useful concept that has been generically applied to so many situations that it has become difficult to even define. Everyone wants it, others urge you to get it, you value it when you have it, yet no one is certain exactly what it is or how to make it happen.

Some professionals working in the area of grief and loss have chosen to stop using the word "closure" all together because it has become so confusing. While it seems the actual word choice leaves something to be desired, the fact remains that the concept is valid and plays an important role in addressing the intense emotions of grief.

Closure can be a feeling. Closure can be a fact. Closure can be an event. You may even have had closure, then some new information surfaces after the death that creates new questions or issues. The inability to directly address new concerns can effectively create a new need for closure that may not be possible.

Just as "letting go" means letting go of your old normal and not of your loved one, "closure" means you are only closing loose ends surrounding your loss. Resolving loose ends allows you to remove complications and distractions related to your loss so you can move forward in a less restricted, less burdened, and healthier way.

Closure means different things to different people in different situations. What is right for you may not be right for someone else. Not only the definition is unique to each individual and each situation, but so is the method of achievement.

Chris' Story—Closure Is In the Eye of the Beholder

Chris had an embittered relationship with her father. It seemed holding onto his anger had always been more valuable to him than having a relationship with any of his children. Chris had repeatedly done her best, but the results had been consistently poor.

The day came when the father's death was imminent, and Chris felt obligated to participate in the family's death watch. The man had delivered a lifetime of relentless emotional and physical cruelty to his entire family, and in his final hours he asked for forgiveness.

Without hesitation, Chris responded, "Too little, too late."

Some may be quick to judge Chris harshly in this situation while others may applaud her courage. Until a person has walked in your shoes, who is to say? For Chris, she was being true to herself by refusing to grant a last-minute pardon in exchange for years of abuse.

Chris was sad for the life her father lived, but she was relieved the abuse was finally over. For Chris, her father's death was her closure. For one or more of her siblings, perhaps granting the desired forgiveness may have been their closure. Closure is in the eye of the beholder.

Road Blocks to A New Normal—Lawsuits

If the death you have experienced came with a summons, or if you are choosing to sue someone else as a result of the death of your loved one, expect major delays on your path to creating A New Normal.

Not only do legal battles engulf every aspect of your life, they also keep you completely focused on the death. You will be repeating your story with lawyers, in grueling depositions, in front of a judge and maybe jury, the same story over and over, with the common goal of provoking your most painful emotions. One side will work to discredit you in any way possible while the other works to display your pain and suffering for all to see. You may be required to look at upsetting pictures. You may view painfully familiar articles of clothing or other personal items. You may be exposed to highly disturbing autopsy details.

If you do find yourself involved in a lawsuit, do your best to create a disaster plan, a worst-case scenario defense in case things do not go as you hope. Be sure to consider your financial needs, but focus predominantly on your physical well being. No one ever finished a marathon without pacing themselves, getting plenty of sleep and eating well. The best way to win is to come out with your health in tact, no matter what the judge says. And when it's finally over, know there is more work ahead.

A Giant Step to A New Normal—Funerals

Viewing a newly-dead body leaves no room for doubt about the finality of your situation. Seeing a body professionally "prepared" for a funeral may not have as strong an impact, but it is still very effective in replacing denial with reality. Cremation has become very common as the choice of many, but viewing an urn of ashes can slow the acceptance of the death as your mind wrestles to connect the urn to your loved one.

The one subject that has come up most often in my therapy practice is the decision of whether or not to view the body. This is a decision that must be made quickly and under pressure with no options for a do over. There is no correct answer, but there is a theme in what bereaved people report to me most often.

Many who chose or were not able to view the body later regret this choice and struggle to accept the reality that their loved one is indeed gone. This is especially true if there was a geographical separation that makes it very easy to go on as if nothing has changed. I have also been told by many who were initially reluctant to view the body but changed their minds that they were very glad they did. They report gaining a sense of comfort in seeing their loved one once more, even in this way.

None of this is to suggest those who choose not to view the body, maybe because they "want to remember her the way she was," is a bad or wrong choice. It is simply another choice. Viewing the body of your loved one does not, however, mean that one memory will or can replace a lifetime of memories. At first the death and surrounding events can seem so large it's hard to believe they could ever fade. But, in time, they do, making room for all your memories once again.

Bereavement Groups

Support groups can be a wonderful resource after the initial shock of your loss has passed. These groups can be especially invaluable to parents who have lost children and for people who have lost loved ones through violence. Finding others with whom you can speak openly about your loss can be difficult for those whose lives have been affected by these types of losses.

Some people who attend groups enjoy the socialization, possibly developing friendships with others they relate to more closely because of the shared loss experiences. New members may find it difficult to assimilate into an established group of this type. If you visit a group a few times and are uncomfortable for this or any other reason, trust your feelings and consider another group.

Finding the right group can make all the difference between a positive and a negative bereavement group experience. Consider whether you prefer a peer or a professionally facilitated group. If you are overwhelmed with emotions and too many things to do following your loss, finding and researching information on groups would be a good job for someone who wants to be of help to you. If you do not find the group process helpful, it doesn't mean there is something wrong with you, it just means you haven't found the right fit for you. You may want to consider individual counseling instead, and many people find doing both helpful.

Chapter 6

Big Losses, Little Recognition

Have you ever considered how much of your life has been affected by loss? Do you ever think about what you had to lose or give up in order to make space for something or someone new? Maybe you are surprised to find yourself experiencing feelings you recognize as grief, yet no one close to you has died.

My colleague and I were invited to speak on grief and loss to a large audience of fellow therapists. Some of the participants stayed after the presentation to speak with us directly. One gentleman commented that he did not understand how we were able to work so much with such a difficult subject. We looked at one another somewhat surprised by the question, both turned to the gentleman and in unison said, "It's ALL grief and loss work!"

Breaking Up Is More Than Hard To Do

A divorce is a death. It is the loss of a dream you once held sacred. It is the end of the way of life as you have known it. Perhaps it is the deconstruction of an intact family that is now a divorced family, a change that will affect generations to come.

Many single-again people report multiple levels of loss. Often coupled friends disappear, as if divorce is a contagious disease they don't want to catch. You may find in-laws who have always been "family" taking sides or simply becoming more distant and less available.

Depending on values within your own family regarding divorce, you could find yourself judged and shunned by your own relatives.

If you were the spouse served unwanted legal papers, the pain and humiliation of your loss on top of the involuntary life changes you are facing can be beyond overwhelming. If you were the spouse serving divorce papers, you may have feelings of uncertainty about your decision, remorse for pain the other partner or your children may be experiencing, or fear of the unknown you are facing. Even if the split was mutual and was handled with the utmost respect and dignity, a divorce is sad—an ending so very different from the way things began.

Loss Competition

A not-so covert battle has rumbled on forever as to which is worse, being widowed or being divorced? That's quite a competition. Who is qualified to judge? What is the answer? There is no relevant comparison, only opinions based on individual experiences.

It's only normal to compare losses of all kinds. You compare your own losses from one to another, your losses that may be similar to someone else's in an effort to gain understanding and clarity. Comparing the pain and suffering related to a loss to see whose is the biggest and the baddest is a contest no one wins.

A New Normal Tip

Give yourself permission and time to grieve for the loss of your relationship. If well-meaning friends want to play matchmaker or drag you to the nearest bar, it's okay to decline or suggest a movie instead. Give serious consideration to taking several months or even a year off from romance. Allow yourself time to look back and process your thoughts and feelings, and time to allow your heart to mend and open again when it's ready. Just as a literal death takes time to assimilate, to establish A New Normal, so does the death of a relationship. A quick test to determine if you are ready to start dating yet is to ask yourself: Would I want to date me right now? There's your answer!

Loss of Financial Well Being

Loss of Job

It doesn't matter if you lost your job through no fault of your own, the impact can still be devastating. You are faced with the need to find another job when you may have been perfectly happy with the one you had. You may suffer financial hardship with time off between jobs, or you may find yourself forced to accept a position for less money than you were making before. In a tough economy, you may struggle to find any job, when having no job is simply not an option.

If you lost your job because you were fired, there is typically an additional layer of trauma to address. You may be angry, embarrassed, ashamed, frightened, depressed, to name only a few of the typical emotions. Finding new work is likely even more challenging in this situation.

A New Normal Tip

Fake it until you make it. It's easy to get discouraged after you lose a job for any reason, but giving up cannot be an option. The best way not to get hired when you do make it to an interview is to present yourself as down, hopeless, desperate, or worse—angry. Worrying is wasted energy when you have work to do.

Loss of Career

A career is something you choose carefully, study and learn about to gain expertise, and work hard to grow and develop. It is a reflection of your personality and how you likely introduce yourself in public. A career can be a dream realized. Is it any wonder that losing a career through industry obsolescence, forced retirement, or any other involuntary means is such a life-altering event?

Age seems to play a major role in how careers are managed today. Younger professionals have entered the workforce expecting to have multiple careers while older Americans more likely expected to have only one. New career fields are blossoming as never before, especially in technical fields. These more recent changes again favor the younger professionals who have been educated more recently, reflecting an education that is more in sync with the current job market. The result is that managing careers today tends to be more challenging for older professionals.

A New Normal Tip

Keep looking forward for momentum and back only for foundation. The guaranteed way to shut down your listeners, and your credibility, is to give the "This Is the Way We Used to Do It," or the "Listen to My Impressive Credentials" speeches. You may be right, but you may also end up unemployed. Get curious. Stay interested. Keep learning.

Loss of Business

If you owned your own business and that business was closed because of financial failure, or taken over for any reason against your will, the loss can be crippling on every possible level.

Your business is not who you are as a person, but it is an entity you nurtured into reality from only a vision—your vision. It is a relationship. What you grew and likely hoped to sell some day for a sizeable profit to create a cozy retirement nest egg has disappeared in a puff of smoke.

It may not be fair, and it sure isn't easy, but it's time to write another business plan. You did it before, so you know how to do it again. You may want to change careers, retire, open a different new business, relocate, hire an expert to help you, go back to school to learn new or enhance existing skills. The sky is the limit and the goal is to choose your direction deliberately and purposefully. Get excited about your future again.

A New Normal Tip

Create your "What Next Plan." Just as buying or starting a business is never a surprise, neither is a business closing. Your best line of defense is to start early to create your "What Next Plan." If your initial plan is nothing more than ideas and busy tasks scribbled on a napkin, beginning to envision a new future can make the difference between positive forward thinking and sinking into a depression just when you need your motivation most.

When major corporations make large reductions in workforces, they avoid making announcements on a Friday. Sending newly unemployed workers out the door with such disturbing news to face a weekend does not bode well. What corporations do instead is announce lay offs or closings first thing on a Monday morning and immediately send the newly-unemployed workers to a busy schedule of benefits counseling, resume writing, and workshops teaching interviewing skills. Staying busy and being productive becomes the new full-time job until replaced by a new paying job!

A New Normal Tip

Always keep your job search records. Whenever you do a job search, you make invaluable networking contacts. You find out what works for you, and you gain job seeking skills and practice. You likely wrote a dozen versions of your resume, each just as difficult to complete as the last—keep them all. Making a record and copies of all your activities can pay off should you find yourself back in the search process again, voluntarily or not.

Work Now, Feel Later

What is common to job loss, career loss, and business loss? They all involve coping with difficult emotions, all likely tap into survival needs, and they all demand you create A New Normal.

What is radically different with these types of losses from the losses we considered earlier is they do not allow you the luxury of taking time to cope with your emotions. Most people need to replace their lost income—fast. Job hunting demands you present only the happiest emotions and most confident attitude, when you may feel neither. If you have a family who depends on you, you likely are in the position of reassuring them when it would be nice if someone reassured you.

Don't be surprised if emotions that necessity required you to shelve come knocking at your door later. They tend to show up only when you feel safe again—safe in your life and safe in your emotions. These were the feelings you had to keep at bay because you had bills to pay and food to buy at the same time you had to find a new job. When the emotions arrive, recognize the fact you can allow them now is validation that you have moved forward in a positive direction. You are no longer in survival mode.

Loss of Youth

Remember when all you ever wanted was to be 18 years old? Then, poof, you were! You blew out the last candles on your cake and announced to your parents, "Now I can do what I want, I'm 18!" Then you asked for the keys to the car and some gas money and permission to stay out late with your friends to celebrate. Losing the fantasy of freedom of life as an adult was just the first of a long list of losses to come.

Loss through Aging

At first it's subtle, then it gets louder, and then it roars. In the beginning, many of the losses of aging are really losses of innocence. To master riding that shiny new bike you learned you must fall down. You only get one first love, typically followed by a first break up.

Before you know it, adolescence is in the rear view mirror and you are a young adult. You work diligently to create the life of your dreams and desires. You create relationships, start families, launch careers. You are young and strong and full of energy. And you are making decisions that will affect you for the rest of your life, for better and for worse.

Every YES decision you make means you said NO to something else. Choose to forego your career to stay home with a young family? You pay the price in years lost to develop your career later. Choose to forego a family now in favor of growing your career? You forfeit the opportunity and perks of being a young parent, or maybe you wait so long you lose the option of ever being a biological parent at all.

Blink your eyes and midlife arrives. Midlife transitions are very real and tend to grab your attention around significant birthdays. A mid-life crisis is an option but not a necessity.

Mid-life is a key time for making a major life review. This is a time to compare your goals and expectations to see how closely the two match, and make adjustments if they don't. You realistically evaluate the time you have left to do all the things you want and hope to do. This is frequently a life stage when marriages must be re-born or end, friendships are re-evaluated with some discarded, old careers may be shed and new ones initiated. Mid-life can be a powerful time of profound change.

Here it comes—the Big Five OH. All the things you got away with physically in your younger days come demanding payment. That high school football injury refuses to leave you alone. All that sun worshipping you did in high school in your cute little bikini has you shopping for wrinkle cream and a good dermatologist. You start buying hormones at the drug store you used to make better on your own and for free. A night of passion may include the help of little blue pills you see marketed on television by silver haired actor couples pretending to be romantic. Maybe you find your nest empty, a major change even if it is a welcome one, and a difficult one if not.

And the "Golden Years" arrive. You don't know how, but they do. You mock the person who came up with the term. You look in the mirror and don't recognize the person looking back. Your body doesn't let you do what you want to do, let alone all the things you used to do. It seems like young people don't take you seriously or even listen to you anymore. You have said good-bye to too many loved ones, and may even strangely find yourself getting used to it.

Loss of Health

Loss of health through illness or injury is probably the most humbling experience a person can ever have. Even the strongest of the strong can find themselves dependent on others for their most basic needs. If you are a person who has always valued having control in your life, finding out how little control you really have can be more than sobering.

Living with physical pain can be the biggest challenge of all. It forces you to make difficult decisions about medications that may help at best and bring miserable side effects at worst. You may never have had a problem with depression before but with chronic pain find yourself battling it now. You may be frustrated with your medical care and our healthcare system, just when you need them most.

Does all this loss seem just too overwhelming? Too depressing? It depends on how you look at it.

When you realize loss has always been part of your life, it doesn't seem quite so daunting. The many losses you experience throughout your personal development bring with them a plethora of gifts and opportunities. Losing a job may open you to the possibilities of an even better job. Feeling you are out of options in one area may push you to a fresh perspective that opens the door to possibilities you had never considered before. Getting healthy again after a serious illness may prompt you to appreciate your health and life in a brand new way.

What Do I Do?

Give yourself credit for all the things you already know about grief and loss. Understand that new losses create new experiences and a need for new awareness. The learning is ongoing throughout your life.

Take the path of least resistance. The less you fight, the more you accept your situation and your emotions, the smoother your journey will be. Make peace with loss.

Find or create SOMETHING to look forward to every day. No matter how insignificant, make sure that when you wake up tomorrow there is something you can get excited about. It can be a movie you've been waiting to see, lunch with a friend, writing a fresh version of your resume, starting a new class or learning a new skill. The possibilities are endless. Find what works for you.

Know you always have choices. You may feel trapped, but you always have options. You can choose how you feel, how you react, and how you handle adversity. What is one thing you can do right now to change your present reality into a new one? Just your thoughts have the power to change your current situation, not to mention your actions. Create the reality you want and deserve to have.

If forgiveness is needed, start first by forgiving yourself. For many, this is the most difficult task of all. Often people are surprised when they realize how harshly they judge themselves. Hindsight too often includes regrets for deeds done or not done, for words uttered or never said. You will never know what might have happened had your situation been different, but you do know being hard on yourself doesn't make a difficult situation any better.

Forgive others when you are ready. People often shame themselves into forgiveness, believing they SHOULD forgive, or feeling guilty because they can't forgive. Real forgiveness can require hard work and time. Forgive when you are genuinely willing and able to forgive from your heart, and not a minute sooner.

Know genuine forgiveness is about freedom. Forgiving someone does not mean you have a new best friend. It doesn't even mean you have to talk with the person, makes amends, or necessarily ever see them again. Forgiveness means you release obsessive thoughts about the person who hurt you. There is no longer a desire to get even, punish, or think about what you wish you had said or done differently, in fact you may no longer think of them at all. Forgiving means you have put the past where it belongs and can head toward your future unencumbered. Forgiveness is something you do for *you*.

Live NOW with passion and gratitude. Tomorrow can only give you hope and direction; yesterday nothing but memories and lessons. Today gives you an amazing grand buffet of endless possibilities. Choose wisely because the choices you make today become the reality of your tomorrow.

Talking about grief and loss experiences, obtaining valuable new information, getting answers to tough questions often stirs up a whole new set of questions. We've covered a lot of material so far, but we're not done yet. Next we look at questions you may still have that have not yet been answered.

Chapter 7

Questions Answered, Myths Dispelled

Just as the subject of grief and loss is endless, so are the questions that go with it. This chapter addresses some of the most commonly asked questions grieving people bring to therapy in their search for answers, clarification, and peace of mind.

Question: Am I crazy?

If you weren't crazy before your loss, you probably aren't crazy after—you just feel like it. Dial the phone and forget who you're calling? Drive down the road and no clue where you are going? Find a bottle of shampoo in the fridge—twice? That's typical grief behavior.

Most newly bereaved people find themselves confused by their own behaviors in the early days of grief. It's like you don't even know yourself anymore. You wonder if you have lost your mind, but more importantly, you wonder if you will ever get it back.

Your brain is working overtime to assimilate the changes coming at you faster than you can process. It's as if you are taking a tennis lesson and the ball machine goes haywire, slinging so many balls at you so fast that all you can do is duck. Your body is physically depleted and your mind is on overload, even the simplest tasks become difficult. This immediate after effect will pass, but there are things you can do to help yourself make the process a little easier.

Caring for yourself, even if you don't feel like it, is the first line of defense. Get some rest, however and wherever you can. Eat some nourishing food while avoiding sugary desserts that give you a short mood boost, only to leave you feeling worse all too soon. And (dare I say it) get some exercise—even just a short walk in fresh air can calm some of the noisiest of heads. Taking care of yourself as your top priority will help you regain your focus as quickly as possible, and it goes a long way in helping you face the difficult days ahead.

Question: What is the fastest way to get through all these emotions?

There is no fast way, quick way or easy way. The best way through it is to do it. Let how you feel be your gauge rather than the days on a calendar. Know that it is not just okay to experience your emotions, it is healthy and it is normal. Your heart knows how to grieve, even if your mind is reeling. Trust your body to show you the way.

Practice checking in with yourself often by frequently asking, "What do I need right now?" If the answer is, "I need rest," then rest. If the answer is, "I need to be alone," be alone. If the answer is, "I need to be around my loved ones," go find them. Start with these little questions in the beginning and tackle the big questions only when you must and when you can.

Question: It's been two weeks; shouldn't I be "over it" by now?

The reality of your loss may just be starting to sink in at two weeks. Expecting yourself to be "over it" is unrealistic and may make you feel even worse than you already feel. Expect the first year to be the most difficult as you work to create A New Normal, and consider removing the term "over it" from your vocabulary. If others around you use the term, ignore them.

Question: Is there something wrong with me if I don't express my emotions openly?

Keeping your emotions and expression of them private is simply one way of coping that is neither right nor wrong. Grief expressed in private is just as valid as grief expressed in public.

Unfortunately, some people are quick to judge when they see emotions they consider to be too much or too little, as if they wrote the official rule book on the right way to express emotions. Do not let yourself be caught up in the expectations of others who have their own agendas. Be true to yourself and to your own feelings, feelings that you know can and do change from one minute to the next.

Question: Should I take medication to help me cope with the strain and pressure caused by my loss?

Some people avoid medications or any type of mind-altering substances when they are grieving, choosing to feel the full range of their emotions without interference. They are not being brave, and they are not being foolish, they are simply grieving people making the choice that is right for them.

Choosing to see your physician for short term medications to help manage your initial reactions to your loss is another option. This is a very personal choice with no one right or wrong solution. If you do choose to use medication, be careful to keep in mind how easy it is to make mistakes or feel confused when you are in the initials throws of grief. It would be easy to forget if you took a pill and accidentally took two or forgot to take an important medication at all. This might be a good time to ask a family member for help or temporarily use a daily pill dispenser box to help you keep on track.

Make sure you understand what you are taking, the correct dosage, and when to take it. Know the side effects you may experience. Ask your doctor how long you should take the medication, what you should do if you experience an adverse reaction, and be sure to check for interactions with any other medications you may be taking. By the way, popping a pill or two a friend offers you from their prescription in your time of distress? Not such a good idea.

If you have been diagnosed previously with some type of mental health condition and use medication regularly to help manage your symptoms, the extreme stress of grieving may require a re-evaluation. If at all possible, see the same medical provider who treated you before your loss, someone who knows you and your history, so an accurate assessment can be made. Be sure to advise your doctor that you are grieving a significant loss as this can affect your physical as well as your emotional well being.

Question: They say "time heals all wounds." Can't I just wait it out?

Time alone cannot heal. Time does create distance from your loss that can help you to adjust and re-establish your routines, but this is not the path to recovery. Working to create A New Normal with the help of time is a healthy way to cope with loss, instead of just waiting for some imaginary day when your loss will magically no longer be an issue.

Question: I can't stop crying. What's wrong with me?

In the early days following a painful loss, it may seem like you will never stop crying. Grieving people often say they are afraid if they start crying they will never be able to stop. As powerful as the feelings may be, the reality does not support the theory. Have you ever heard of someone crying for years without stopping?

Grief can be a funny thing. You can be sobbing and choking to breathe one minute, then all of a sudden feel kind of hungry the next. The quick change may even startle you, leaving you once again wondering if you really are losing your mind. In fact, this is your body's built-in self protection early warning system telling you, "That's enough for now." Let your inner wisdom guide you on this difficult journey.

The mantra in my therapy practice is, WE HEAL THROUGH LAUGHTER AND TEARS. Let your tears do their job, and know they will not stay any longer than they are needed.

Question: I haven't cried at all. What's wrong with me?

You are just as normal in your grief as the person who feels they can't stop crying. You may be in shock. You may just be so overwhelmed you are doing your best to simply function. You may also be busy taking care of everyone else so there has been no time to take care of you—yet. Be patient with yourself. The emotions are there, they are just waiting for the time when you are ready for them.

Question: How will I know if I need professional help?

There is a difference between needing and wanting to get professional help. If several weeks have passed and you find you are unable to resume simple tasks and routines, you may want to consider getting professional help from a qualified mental health provider. On the other hand, if you simply feel the need to talk with someone outside of your grief community, someone who is objective and supportive, then you may find talking with a professional experienced in grief work very beneficial.

If you are looking for a therapist skilled in grief and loss work, start by asking those around you if there is someone they can recommend. If you are shopping from a list of unknown providers, begin by calling and asking for a brief phone interview in order to make your selection. Make sure you find a licensed professional. A license is designed to protect the public by proving the practitioner has completed minimum required training, testing, internships, and participates in ongoing education. Any licensed professional should be happy to share their credentials with you, and the physical license should be posted where it is easily seen.

Too many people have come to me for therapy because another therapist could not contain his or her own emotions when hearing about an upsetting loss. The job of a therapist is not to join you in your emotions, but to listen with compassion and provide witness to your story and your experience. If you feel like you need to take care of your therapist's feelings, it's time for a new therapist. Find the right person for you.

Question: Talking about it only makes me feel worse. Why shouldn't I just push my thoughts and feelings aside and get on with my life?

Staying busy and not dwelling on your grief can be an option, and it can be helpful at times. However, staying busy to avoid your grief does not mean you are getting on with your life.

Rejecting your thoughts and feelings does not mean they are not still there; it just means they are operating under the surface and away from conscious awareness. Think about a computer virus that is corrupting your system without you even knowing. The virus is still there. The longer you wait, the more damage it does, the harder it is to clean it up.

Question: If I take my focus off my loved one's death, I will lose the only connection I have left. Why wouldn't I hold on to my grief?

It's actually the other way around. When you stay focused on death, you cannot be focused on the bigger story—life. When you stay locked in your grief, you deny yourself any feelings of joy from happier times. And when you hold onto your pain, it means every single time you think of the person you loved and lost, your pain begins all over again.

Letting go of the person's death does not mean you are letting go of the person. Letting go of the death allows you to celebrate their entire life, cherish the time you had together, and bring your loved one back into your life in a whole new way through the many memories you shared. They may be physically gone from your life, but in this way they can very much live on in your heart for the rest of your days.

Question: I thought I was doing okay but now I'm worse. Am I having a grief relapse?

Grief is not an illness or an addiction, conditions where recovery may include relapses. Grief is an emotion. It comes in waves— sometimes a lot and sometimes a little. The feelings will pass, and the feelings will likely return multiple times—both are normal in the grief process. You may be okay, but you may also still be grieving—possibly at the same time.

Question: What is the difference between grieving and mourning?

Grieving means you are experiencing the feelings of grief, such as distress, suffering and sorrow. Mourning refers to the physical act of grieving, the outward signs of grief as in attending a funeral or putting flowers on a grave.

Question: Is it true there is no right or wrong way to grieve?

Grief is a feeling and there is no right or wrong way to feel. Grief is only one of many emotions including happy, sad, angry, and glad. We certainly enjoy some feelings over others, but they are all nothing more and nothing less than feelings that come and go over the course of time.

Unlike grief, however, there can healthy and unhealthy ways to express feelings, unhealthy ways to mourn—to act or behave. Abusing drugs and/or alcohol to medicate or numb difficult emotions would be unhealthy. Raging at drivers in other vehicles for little or no reason to avoid facing your own anger would be unhealthy.

A note of clarification seems appropriate here about the difference between anger and rage. Anger is a normal, healthy, human emotion we all experience from time to time. Rage is not a normal, healthy, human emotion. Rage is anger infected, out of control, and toxic. Rage is when people and things get hurt and broken through actions, words and deeds. If you find yourself raging, or see someone you love raging, professional intervention would be wise to prevent further escalation and to promote a return to good mental health.

Question: Is it normal to be angry with the person who died for leaving you? If I'm not angry, does it mean I am in denial?

You absolutely do NOT have to be angry with your loved one for dying, but you MIGHT be angry with your loved one for dying. It's possible to even be grateful for a loved one's death, not because you are glad they died, but you are glad they are released from suffering. Wanting what is best for another person, even if it brings you pain, is what it means to truly love someone.

Question: I feel guilty when I laugh. How will I know when it's okay to laugh again? Will it ever be okay to laugh again?

Just as crying is "okay," so is laughing. You may even find yourself doing them both at the same time. You might be startled the first time a real laugh escapes your mouth, perhaps shocked it's even possible amidst so many dark emotions. Embrace laughter. Share your funny stories of your loved one and let everyone join in. *We heal through laughter and tears—both!*

Question: I have grieved the loss of people close to me who have died, but nothing has ever devastated me like the loss of my pet. Is there something wrong with me that my pet dying is having a greater impact on me than when people in my life have died?

Believe it or not, this is the question I am asked most often in and out of my professional setting. For those of us who love our animals and consider them part of our families, the loss of a pet IS devastating. Rather than trying to rank which death is more significant, consider the impact of your loss on your every day life.

Your pet gave you constant unconditional love in a way no human ever can or will. You were together every single day, but never tired of one another. You shared frequent physical contact and affection, for some the only regular affection received. You were greeted at the door each time you walked in as if you were the Grand Ruler of the World, even if you only went out to get the mail. When they are gone, their absence permeates every aspect of your entire life.

If you are not an animal lover and are reading this in an effort to understand someone you love who is grieving the loss of a pet, here is the truth. You don't have to understand. No one ever completely understands another person's loss. Just listen and be supportive, and above all else, do NOT try to fix the problem. It isn't a problem to be solved. It is grief to be felt.

Question: My friend, who I care very much about, is grieving deeply for the loss of a close loved one. What can I do to help my friend?

First, stop talking and start listening. It is not possible to talk and listen at the same time. Second, don't worry about saying something brilliant or saying the right thing, just keep listening. Forget the silly almost obligatory phrase, "Let me know if there's anything I can do." Just do it. Go wash their dishes. Take their dirty laundry, deliver it back clean, and don't worry if they even noticed. Pick up their kids from school, feed them, make sure they do their homework, and deliver them home bathed in their pajamas. With words, less is more. With actions, more is more.

Question: Why doesn't Chapter 4 on loss by relationship include a section for parents who lose children?

The focus of this book is to help as many people as possible with the losses most if not all of us experience at some time in our lives. I have been honored over the years to work with many grieving parents whose stories are deliberately not included in this book. If there is one thing I have learned, it is that a parent's loss of a child is anything but a common loss, no matter what the age or the cause. It would be impossible to do justice to this subject as a section of a chapter in this book, but many wonderful books are available that do address this type of loss in great detail. I encourage you to read them all, take what works and discard what does not.

Question: If everyone loses someone they love at some point, and if death is just a part of life, why do I feel so alone?

Grieving is lonely. It is private, and it is sacred.

You may share your loss with others, but your grief is unique to only you, as theirs is to them. Even if you have siblings and you share the loss of the same parent, you each experience your loss differently. Your experiences are individualized by your particular relationship to your parent, your birth order, your gender, your age at the time of your loss, your spiritual beliefs, and so many more aspects of who you are as a person. Others may effectively empathize, but no one truly knows exactly how you feel.

Grief is often felt the deepest in the private moments when no one else is around. You may even feel isolated in your own private bubble when in fact you are surrounded by a noisy crowd of people. Think about having seen a grieving person on television, a too-private moment captured by some soul-less camera, played over and over on public news programs for the world to see. Just as we are voyeurs, deliberate or by accident, there is a sense of shame for violating something so incredibly personal, private, and raw.

And, yes, grief is sacred. It is the most primal, genuine expression of your very deepest emotions. It is you at your most vulnerable. It is one of the most intensely intimate connections you may ever have with someone who means so much, and who is missed so sorely. The many powerful rituals that surround the death of a loved one are intended to honor and celebrate the person's life, but nothing celebrates life more than the love shared between two people. This is us at our most human, us at our very best.

Chapter 8

Helplessness to Resilience—
The Author's Story

The Background

I spent nearly two decades climbing the Fortune 500 corporate ladder as a Human Resources professional. Achieving impressive titles, corner offices, and a salary in the top 3 percent earning bracket for women in the United States, by most people's standards, I was successful.

I enjoyed my work, and as a single parent I appreciated the financial security it provided for my family. There was never a moment to think about the effects of my choices—there was only one direction and that was straight ahead.

You don't notice when "Golden Handcuffs" are slipped onto your wrists. These are the increasing perks you get that make leaving an employer foolish at first, and nearly impossible on your terms later. At some point you realize they are there, but you not only like them, you want more. Then, you start to realize doors are closing on other opportunities, and those shiny invisible bracelets begin to get a little tighter and a little less shiny. Still, you don't really pay much attention to your "Golden Handcuffs" until they cut, you begin to bleed, and you feel trapped.

Disillusionment began to set in for me as the further my career advanced, the less personal satisfaction I got from the work I was doing.

I lived on airplanes, sat in tedious meetings, slept in hotel beds more often than my own, and jumped through one political hoop after another. I found my own integrity out of sync too many times, and that created inner turmoil I could not effectively ignore.

I knew for a long time that some day I wanted and needed to be self employed. I also couldn't help but notice in my early 40's there were few co-workers over 55 to be found. I'd have been a fool not to know some day it would be my turn, and I began envisioning my future independence long before it was ever a real option.

When my sons became emancipated young adults, I found myself with a new sense of freedom. For the first time, I could take real risks. If things went poorly I would harm no one but myself, and I did a crazy thing. I accepted an assignment to open a large Southwest business operating out of Las Vegas. This was going to be fun, and fun was something I definitely needed to add to my life. Or, at least, that was the plan.

Everything that could go wrong quickly went very wrong. It started with a massive earthquake in California that damaged the profitability of the business, and it all went downhill from there. The business never had a chance and the future was easy to predict. Management heads were rolling every direction. It was time to make another change, and fast.

I aggressively launched my next job search. In no time, I connected with my dream job and it looked like I was headed back east for my next corporate gig. I should have been excited, but I was tired of moving, I was travel weary, and I was sick of making friends I had to leave. I had fallen in love with the desert and wanted badly to stay, but there really seemed to be no choice. Little did I know the change headed my way, or just how wrong I could be.

From Helplessness...

The obnoxious phone jarred me awake too early on the morning of December 24, 1994. I figured it had to be someone calling from the

Eastern Time Zone because it happened so often and was always annoying. I remember swearing to myself when I moved back to the east I would never be so inconsiderate of Pacific Time Zone people again.

The call was from an Ohio relative letting me know she had received a call from a local hospital. She said my mother had been taken there by ambulance, but she had no idea why. Hospital? Ambulance?

I was baffled. I'd spoken with Mom on the phone the previous evening. She had taken the day off work to finish last-minute Christmas shopping and said she didn't feel well. Her back had been bothering her and treatment had not relieved the discomfort, but there were no other apparent issues with her health. We were both tired from holiday stress and agreed to get some rest. I promised to check on her in the morning, and we said, "Good-night." I couldn't even guess how she could be in the hospital, via ambulance no less, only hours later.

I quickly called long distance to the hospital, expecting to get a volunteer giving me some generic status report. Instead, I was immediately connected to the attending physician. What on earth was happening?

The physician was kind, but direct and to the point. She informed me my mother had called for an ambulance, let the Emergency Medical Technicians into her home, and proceeded to have a massive heart attack. She said they "lost her" in the ambulance on the way to the hospital, succeeded in reviving her, and she'd had a second attack that had destroyed the main valve in her heart. She told me my mother was not going to live.

Well, that was just absurd. This had to be some awful mistake. I just talked to Mom and, except for the back ache, she was fine. My mother was young, only 69 years old, and came from a long line of strong women who live and lived forever. She'd never even been in the hospital, other than to give birth decades before. Her own mother as of this writing is 102 and pretty healthy for an old lady.

I was taking the situation seriously, but clearly the physician had to be horribly mistaken.

Being the dutiful daughter who loved her mother very much, I was faced with my first choice. If there was any truth to what I was being told, I needed to be my mother's voice as I had promised to do. Would I honor her wishes made so clear to me in the past, or would I choose what I wanted which was not to lose my mother? In my mind, there was no choice as I said, "My mother did not want any heroic measures ever taken on her behalf. I do not want her to be placed on life support." There, I said it.

Ignorance isn't always bliss. Without hesitation, the physician informed me that not only was my mother already on life support, but that if it was disconnected, she would immediately die. I was then slapped with my next choice when she asked, "What do you want?"

What do I want? What do I *want*? I want to go to the bathroom since I was just so rudely jerked awake! I want some caffeine, a whole vat of caffeine! I want to go back to sleep and end this awful nightmare, wake up and start this day over again! This was not happening.

As calmly as I could, I told the physician to do whatever tests she needed to do so we could make a fully-informed decision. I told her while she completed all the tests, I would be on an airplane to get there as fast as I could, and allow the family time to gather. She agreed but followed with the warning, "Don't expect your mom to be alive when you get here." This woman sure wasn't cutting me any slack. I'd say I was speechless, but I told her the only thing I knew to say, the only thing I knew to be true. "She'll wait for me."

I went into achievement-oriented auto pilot. Shock really does come in handy sometimes. I made arrangements to vanish instantly with no idea when I would return. I slung clothes into a suitcase and froze when the next choice gave me a sour look at my situation. Did I pack an outfit appropriate for a funeral, my mother's funeral? Knowing the one thing my mother was most proud of in her entire life was her children, I made my wardrobe choice for her. I packed an outfit I was to wear only one more time.

I won't attempt to describe the flight from Vegas to Cleveland; I'm not sure I could. Nothing was real. I got into my rental car and somehow an hour later walked into the hospital just before midnight.

I had no idea what to expect. It was so hushed, so quiet. There were Christmas decorations everywhere. I tiptoed into the Coronary Care Unit and was amazed when I was happily greeted by multiple medical people calling me by name, saying they knew I'd just flown in from Las Vegas, talking as if they'd known me forever. My mother was alive. They took me into see her, and there were those big brown eyes that just sparkled the minute she saw me. My mother waited for me.

I visited for only the few minutes allowed and left the hospital to head for my home away from home, my aunt and uncle's house. Amazingly, driving through a city I was born, raised and lived in for 30 years, I got lost, really lost. I'm still not sure exactly how I finally arrived at my destination.

Christmas Day was spent with family, short visits in and out with Mom who actually seemed to be doing better. The staff was encouraging as the day went on, in my mind confirming my gene pool theory as fact—we are strong women who live forever. We got the encouraging news that Mom would be moved out of CCU to a regular room in the morning. Feeling hopeful and a little more relaxed, we all realized how hungry and exhausted we were and went to enjoy a late holiday feast while Mom rested.

Then, it happened again. I had barely fallen asleep, complete with a too full stomach, when the hateful ring of the phone woke the household in the very early morning hours of December 26. It was the hospital. They said, "Come now."

Some day I may forgive my uncle for driving so slow, for his determination to get us to the hospital safely on snowy roads. Half way there, I knew it no longer mattered. I knew the moment my mother was gone.

I jumped out of the car before it stopped in the hospital parking lot and I ran. The elevator doors opened for me almost as if by magic, and the staff was waiting for me as I walked off. They shared the news that was not news. They said things I didn't understand, things that really didn't matter anymore, anyway. Their words were a garbled mess and all I could do was nod my head, indicating I understood when I didn't understand at all.

I walked into the room alone. There were those same brown eyes, only now looking anything but alive. I knew I should close them, but I just couldn't do it. I touched her arm that was cool but still warm at the same time. It was immediately clear to me—this was not my mother. This was my mother's body. It looked so small. I didn't know it was possible to hurt so much, or how I could go on if it didn't stop. I didn't think I would ever be able to breathe again.

I am fortunate to look like my mother, but in that moment the similarity brought anything but comfort. I was seeing my own death on top of my mother's. I realized how little time I really have left, and how precious every minute really is. My own life review flew through my mind with clarity I had never experienced before, and my New Normal began to form. I vowed in that moment to experience every single emotion in honor of my amazing mother and this tremendous loss. Then I went to throw up.

After the funeral and the obligatory dinner, I went back into the desperately-needed safety of my aunt and uncle's home. I needed to just sit in a chair and do nothing. But, another surprise was waiting for me when I arrived instead. There it was—an overnight package straight from Corporate America, MY Corporate America. Inside the package was a stack of papers with a note from my boss on top. He wanted to know if I'd be able to get my report done and submitted on time.

I would say that this was my next big choice, but in all honesty, I think the choice made itself. I got the report done and in on time, and I began my exit strategy.

I withdrew from the new job opportunity. I applied and was accepted into graduate school. Seven months later, I left my job, and I left my corporate career. I planted roots in the desert where some amazing things grow when you least expect it.

... To Resilience

I have never once regretted my decisions that led me to this day. I tore through graduate school in record time. I served internships in simple little community clinics, so different from where I'd been. It was so much fun to be learning again. I was doing the work that I loved in a setting that mattered and with people determined to make a better life for themselves.

It will come as no surprise that I began to work with grief and loss cases early in my new career, or that I never stopped. I launched my solo private practice in 1998, and I love my work as much or more today as I did then. Today, I define what success means to me instead of allowing others to do it for me. Today, the definition of success starts with happiness. Today, I am successful.

I still miss my mom all these years later. I have never completely run out of tears, but I did work through the pain, and I did breathe again. The sadness slowly faded and was replaced with an acceptance that allows me to have her with me always. She was never a big fan of therapy, so I wonder what she would think of her daughter, the psychotherapist. I wonder what she would say about her six amazing adult grandchildren or her adorable four little great grandchildren. I really wonder what she would say about menopause!

Not surprisingly, there have been more losses in my life along the way—each unique, each devastating in it's own right. My most recent loss was literally as I was writing Chapter 4 of this book. I was sitting at the kitchen table, writing some notes late on a Sunday, when I had to rush my 8-year-old Wheaten Terrier to the animal hospital. She was fine and three weeks later cancer took her from me, and the world lost the best therapy dog ever.

I found myself faced with another choice, once again born out of pain. Feeling saturated with loss, part of me wanted to just "delete" this whole manuscript and never talk about it again. Ironically (or intuitively, maybe), I'd been stuck for weeks unable to write a decent version of the section on pet loss. I came home without my girl, I sat down, and we wrote it together in a matter of minutes. I knew I had to keep writing.

I miss each of my loved ones I have lost so very much. I do not hesitate to say that a part of me I will never get back went with each of them. But, a part of them I cherish and hold closely in my heart has stayed with me as well, and I will never let go. Whether I shared DNA with those I have lost or not, this was and is my family. My life has been richer because of the family I was given and the family I have chosen. I wouldn't want it any other way.

Conclusion

What you have just read was a whole lot of information crammed into a very little book. The goals were to help you understand at least one thing you didn't understand before, to lighten your pain even just the slightest, and to do both as quickly as possible.

We needed to cover as much territory as we could in as little time as possible. The text needed to be pragmatic, straight forward, honest, and user-friendly for people looking for and needing answers NOW. The challenge was to address the universal experience of loss at the same time respect the unique experience of each reader. And it needed to deeply honor the very personal experiences of the people whose stories were shared.

Armed with a custom roadmap on how to create A NEW NORMAL, your new normal, hopefully you now have a sense of direction. Each step may not be clear, but you know you will figure them out as you go. You have proven tools available to you to help you along the way, tools that have worked for other grieving people who have survived their losses. You now know how to separate fact from fiction.

Today you vow to trust yourself to know what is best for you first, and listen to others second, including all the things you read in this book. Take what works and pitch what doesn't. You are the boss. Acknowledge that grief and loss have always been a part of your life, so learning to live with them not only makes sense, it is necessary.

And now you know you aren't stuck or trapped or out of options. You have choices. You have many choices. The question is what will you do with them, starting today?

About the Author

Darlene Cross is a Licensed Marriage & Family Therapist working in her own private practice. She works with individuals,
couples, families and small businesses in a generalized setting with
a long term focus on grief and loss cases.

In 1996, after 17 years as a Human Resources professional with
General Electric, Cross made a mid-life career change out of the
corporate world. After earning a Masters in Counseling from the
University of Nevada, Las Vegas, she entered the world of mental
health care.

She is the mother of two grown sons and the grandmother of
four young grandchildren. She lives in Henderson, Nevada, where
she devotes herself to spoiling her adorable canine kids. When she
isn't busy being a therapist or working in her family business, you
can find her in the ring at a dog show with her Polish Lowland
Sheepdog, Leksy.